Quick Tips For SAFE and SUCCESSFUL Money Making

. . . .

1. Always get permission from your parents to do ANY of the 76 ways to make money.
2. When going door to door, bring a cell phone and make sure to always keep your parents updated as to where you are.
3. Never go in a home without letting your parents know what house number and street you are at.
4. Make sure to check in frequently so your parents know you are safe.
5. Have your parents check with your local city for needed permits, licenses, etc.
6. Keep track of any money spent for materials.
7. Keep track of all time spent planning, preparing, and working your money making idea.
8. Use the attached work sheet to calculate how much money you made.

76 WAYS

For Kids To Make Money

Amy Beckstead

Illustrator, Bailey Chatterton

BALBOA.
PRESS

A DIVISION OF HAY HOUSE

Balboa Press books may be ordered through booksellers or by contacting:

Balboa Press
A Division of Hay House
1663 Liberty Drive
Bloomington, IN 47403
www.balboapress.com
1 (877) 407-4847

Because of the dynamic nature of the Internet, any web addresses or
links contained in this book may have changed since publication and may
no longer be valid. The views expressed in this work are solely those
of the author and do not necessarily reflect the views of the publisher,
and the publisher hereby disclaims any responsibility for them.

The author of this book does not dispense medical advice or prescribe
the use of any technique as a form of treatment for physical, emotional,
or medical problems without the advice of a physician, either directly
or indirectly. The intent of the author is only to offer information
of a general nature to help you in your quest for emotional and
spiritual well-being. In the event you use any of the information in
this book for yourself, which is your constitutional right, the author
and the publisher assume no responsibility for your actions.

Any people depicted in stock imagery provided by Thinkstock are
models, and such images are being used for illustrative purposes only.
Certain stock imagery © Thinkstock.

Print information available on the last page.

ISBN: 978-1-5043-4217-9 (sc)
ISBN: 978-1-5043-4218-6 (e)

Balboa Press rev. date: 10/19/2015

Contents

Quick Tips For Safe And Successful Money Making..... I

1. Collecting Cans 1
2. Washing Cars, Detailing Cars, & Waxing Cars 2
3. Neighborhood Carnival..3
4. Homework Hall 4
5. Door To Door Taking Out Trash 5
6. Walking Kids To And From School, To
   A Bus Stop, or An After School Activity 6
7. Yard Work..6
8. Walking Dogs 7
9. Paper Route 7
10. Build and Sell Dog Houses..8
11. Fix Bikes...9
12. Build Bike Jumps, Skate Board Ramps,
    and Rails 10
13. Mother's Helper!...11
14. Mani/Pedi Parties 12
15. Pick Up Dog Poop.. 13
16. Clean Out Litter Boxes 14
17. Wrap Christmas Gifts 15
18. Collect Juice Containers or Soda Tabs
    and Make Bags, Purses, Bracelets, and
    Other Great Things....................................... 16
19. Painting House Numbers, Curb Side...................... 17
20. Build Tree Houses 18
21. Painting Fences... 19
22. Teach a Skill, Sport, or Talent 20

23. Make Suckers and Sell Them at School or In The Neighborhood 21

24. Collecting and Selling Used Golf Balls 21

25. Picking and Selling Fruit From Fruit Trees! 22

26. Bake and Sell Pies For Thanksgiving 23

27. Make Christmas Wreaths and Sell Them 24

28. Grow and Sell Pumpkins for Halloween 24

29. Refinish Old Wooden Boats and Sell On-line 25

30. Create a Neighborhood Haunted House 25

31. Waxing and Tuning Snowboards 26

32. Build Specialty Furniture Out of Skateboards, Snowboards, or Ski's 26

33. Snow Tube and Snow Sled Rentals 27

34. Hang and Take Down Christmas Lights 28

35. Baby Sitting 29

36. Cleaning Houses 30

37. Computer Tech Tutor 30

38. Build Doll Houses 31

39. Neighborhood Theater 32

40. Make Book Marks 33

41. Water Indoor Plants 34

42. Face Painting at Birthday Parties or Other Events 35

43. Build Lemonade Stands 36

44. Construction Site Clean Up 37

45. After School Programs 38

46. Brushing/Feeding Horses or Other Animals 38

47. Assistant Coach 38

48. Personal Life Guard 39

49. Take Little Kids Christmas or Special Occasion Shopping 39

50. Weed Bouquets 39
51. Write a Book 40
52. Sell Firewood 40
53. Build Bird Houses 40
54. Build, Paint, Put Together Model Cars
    or Airplanes... 41
55. Parent Paid Education.................................... 41
56. Sell Candy, Water, Drinks, and more at
    Parades, Baseball Games, and Other Events....... 42
57. Water Lawns.. 42
58. Take Pictures and Video's at Children's Events ...43
59. Read Books to Little Kids 44
60. Clean Out Garages 44
61. Patch Boats... 45
62. Refinish Old Bathroom and Kitchen
    Cabinets and Resale On-line 45
63. Build Go-Carts and Sell Them........................ 46
64. Acting/Modeling... 46
65. Neighborhood Newsletter 47
66. Refereeing..47
67. Create your own You-Tube Channel.................. 48
68. Forex Market/Stock Market 49
69. Aerating Lawns.. 50
70. Washing Windows... 50
71. Gas Station/Store Runner.............................. 51
72. House Sitting... 52
73. Kid Olympics.. 53
74. Simple Mechanics 53
75. On-line Store... 53
76. Morning Car Warm-Up/Window Scraper............ 54

1. Collecting Cans

Ask your neighbors or local businesses, to save their soda cans for you. Once a week go with a wagon and collect them. Most communities have recycling centers who pay good money for aluminum, copper, brass, steel, iron, and batteries. You can find these materials everywhere! Get creative, make some money recycling and help Mother Earth at the same time!

2. Washing Cars, Detailing Cars, & Waxing Cars

This takes minimal equipment and can be done door to door or set up at a local gas station. The secret to a good carwash is to rinse the car well after being washed, and dry it fast! For detailing, use a clean, unused small paint brush or tooth brush to get in the small crevasses to dust or clean. Good Luck!

3. Neighborhood Carnival

· ·

This one can be really fun! Create games, rides, entertainment, haunted houses, and anything else you can think of. Sell tickets for each activity over a set period of time, then set days or hours when/where this will be happening. Get creative! Don't forget prizes for the games.

4.   Homework Hall

. . . .

Set up your bedroom, or an area in your home to be a mini classroom. 2-3 days per week, at specific time (3-5 PM), supervise or help the younger kids in the neighborhood with homework. I wish I had a homework hall to send my daughter to when she was growing up. You can have multiple kids at once and run it like a classroom. Simply keep everyone focused and help those who ask. You can even do this one on one or help with specific projects such as science projects or book reports for a bigger fee.

5. Door To Door Taking Out Trash

This idea is great for large apartment or condominium complexes. No one likes running down to the dumpster. Charge by the bag and use a wagon to stack up multiple bags. When the wagon is full, take a trip to the dumpster. Get some regular customers and drop by once or twice a week to make the money!

6. Walking Kids To And From School, To A Bus Stop, or An After School Activity

Most parents are extremely busy and would love to hire a RELIABLE older kid to make sure their kids get to the bus stop safe, to and from school, or to an after school activity.

7. Yard Work

Pull weeds, rake leaves, shovel snow, mow lawns, water lawns, or weed whack.

8. Walking Dogs

Walk dogs for neighbors. Make sure if you take more than one dog at a time the dog owner is okay with it. Some dogs get along with other dogs and some do NOT! Be safe!

9. Paper Route

Check with your local newspaper companies. I did this from age 9-13 on my bike, early in the morning. There are usually afternoon routes too!

10. Build and Sell Dog Houses

. . . .

Go to some newly built homes and ask the General Contractor if you can have excess materials from the home being built. Make sure you get permission first! Use the left over wood, shingles, nails, insulation, etc. to build a dog house. You can find dog house building plans on-line or just get creative. Then paint with a good exterior paint. Market your dog houses door to door or sell them on-line.

11. Fix Bikes

. . . .

There are a few ways to do this great idea. How many broken down bikes sit in the garages just waiting for their parents to find the time to fix them? You can go mobile door to door or set up a shop in your garage. Buy some supplies common to fixing bikes such as tubes, patches, etc. You are ready to open up shop and start getting the kids rolling again on their bikes!

12. Build Bike Jumps, Skate Board Ramps, and Rails

Most the core materials for this can also be found on construction sites. With permission from the General Contractor, grab the materials you need and go to work. This can be fun and very profitable. You can sell these at local skate parks, in the neighborhood, or on-line.

13. Mother's Helper!

Be a Mother's helper for parties, activities, shopping, etc. Moms are always trying to do so much on their own and it would be nice to have a helper at a birthday bash or activity that requires managing multiple kids. Make some flyer's and hand them out in your neighborhood. It may even be cheaper to make business cards. Ask your parents to help!

14. Mani/Pedi Parties

Throw a Mani/Pedi Party for the kids in the neighborhood. Have the kids come with clipped nails and then you can file their nails, paint, and decorate each finger and toe nail. This will be fun and you can make a monthly activity out of it.

15. Pick Up Dog Poop

This might be smelly but very much needed. No one likes to clean up after their dogs so if you can handle this job, there is big money it! I used to pay a boy weekly to stay on top of picking up my dogs poop. Each week he would come at the same time and make his rounds. This way by staying on top of it, it makes it easier for you! And the dog owner gets to enjoy a poo-less yard.

16. Clean Out Litter Boxes

This is needed just like picking up dog poop. Make a weekly visit to your neighbors and clean out litter boxes. This will bring in good money for you, and a nice clean smelling house for the customer.

17. Wrap Christmas Gifts

· ·

This involves a skill level that can deliver a nicely wrapped gift. Christmas time is going to be the busiest season. Make sure you have the customer provide all the materials and labels. Make sure you keep the gifts straight as to who's is who's. :) This works best one customer at a time. That way you don't get the items being wrapped mixed up. Once you do a few batches you'll be an expert at wrapping gifts and you can add your signature creativity.

18. Collect Juice Containers or Soda Tabs and Make Bags, Purses, Bracelets, and Other Great Things

You can find some design ideas on-line or simply use your creativity to make these items. Sell them to friends and family. I loved the swim bag my daughter made out of capri sun containers. It was water proof and perfect for the pool. Try selling these items at Farmer's Markets, Flea Markets, and Yard Sales!

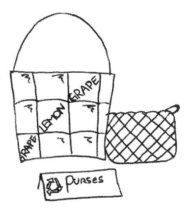

19. Painting House Numbers, Curb Side

Neatly paint the house numbers on the curbs. You will need a number template for this idea, and some cement colored paint for mess ups. Take your time and make it look good. Practice first on some old plywood before you go out. You can place an ad on-line or go door to door. Houses up for sale will be good targets. Everyone wants their home in tip top shape when it's up for sale.

20. Build Tree Houses

Are you good at building tree houses? A safe tree house is very important and if you are good at it, you can offer your services to other kids in the neighborhood. Make sure you have permission from the parents before you start pounding nails.

21. Painting Fences

. . . .

Go door to door and offer to fix, scrape, repair, and paint wooden fences. Wooden fences get worn quickly but can look brand new with a little paint. Make sure you scrape off the old flakes, sand it as needed, and then apply a fresh exterior wood paint to the fence. Take your time and do a good job and all the neighbors will be knocking on your door to give you work!

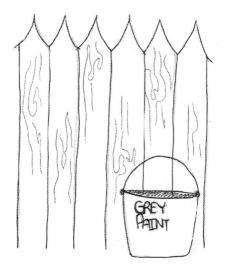

22. Teach a Skill, Sport, or Talent

. . . .

Do you know how to play the piano, a sport, or do something unique? You can teach the basics to young kids in the neighborhood. For an example; a young 5 year old just learning soccer would benefit from an older kid working with her/him to fine tune the basics. This will set the young kids up for great success!

23. Make Suckers and Sell Them at School or In The Neighborhood

. . . .

This can be fun and a big money maker. Use various designs and flavors. Wrap them in clear wrap and sell them at school for big profits. I like cinnamon!

24. Collecting and Selling Used Golf Balls

. . . .

Golf balls are very expensive and the avid golfer loves buying used golf balls. Go search for these balls on the outer fences of golf courses. You can even get permission to collect them from the course before or after hours. Next, clean them and sell them at a stand outside of a local golf course. Also, try buying in bulk from kids who already collected them. This is big money for kids who are willing to do the search.

25. Picking and Selling Fruit From Fruit Trees!

This is a double sided way to make money. Go to your neighbors and offer to pick old pieces of fruit from their tree or on the ground. Charge for this service. Next, ask for permission to keep any good pieces of fruit as you pick the old. Then, keep some for your family and sell the rest at a fruit stand or door to door to other neighbors.

26. Bake and Sell Pies For Thanksgiving

You want to make sure you have a parent helping you with this project. The ingredients, materials, and time will all be apart of your cost. Go door to door and offer for the neighbors to preorder pies for Thanksgiving. I would suggest 2-4 kinds of pies. Collect money with the preorder so you can get the needed materials and plan a time and date to drop off the order!

27. Make Christmas Wreaths and Sell Them

. . . .

Get creative and make Christmas wreaths. Look for pinecones and other natural materials to minimize the cost. Load them up in your wagon and sell them door to door.

28. Grow and Sell Pumpkins for Halloween

. . . .

This idea will have to be started early on in May. Ask your parents for a spot in the garden and plant early on in May for a plump selling season in October. When the time is right, pick the pumpkins, load them up in your wagon and start selling. Buy some pumpkin carving kits in bulk and sell for profit along with your pumpkins.

29. Refinish Old Wooden Boats and Sell On-line

You can find old wooden canoes or fishing boats in local classifieds. Refinish the boats and apply a new coat of paint. Sell online for profit.

30. Create a Neighborhood Haunted House

This idea can be a lot of fun and a lot of work. Most Haunted Houses are for older kids or young adults. Try creating a child friendly haunted house with other activities such as cookie decorating or face painting. Charge per activity or one entry fee.

31. Waxing and Tuning Snowboards

Do you know how to tune up a snowboard? If not, watch some You-tube videos and learn how. I Did! Get the needed materials such as wax, an edger, scraper, and wax iron and set up shop to tune up snowboards or ski's for big money!

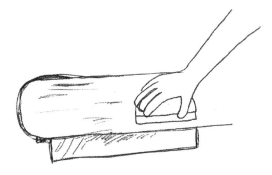

32. Build Specialty Furniture Out of Skateboards, Snowboards, or Ski's

Look in local classifieds and buy cheap snowboards, old skateboards, and ski's. Take these and make furniture out of them such as, chairs, benches, tables, coat racks, beds, shelves, and mirrors. There is no limit to what you can create. Just be sure to charge enough to cover the expenses, and your time. Have fun!

33. Snow Tube and Snow Sled Rentals

. . . .

Go to the most popular snow sledding hill and set up shop. Rent snow sleds and tubes out by the hour or by the trip. If you have something fun to ride, you will even attract customers who have their own sleds. Sell hot chocolate while you're there for extra profit.

34. Hang and Take Down Christmas Lights

This is a triple money maker. Go and offer to hang Christmas Lights for your neighbors, and then after the season is over go and ask to take them down. Lastly, offer to dispose of the old Christmas lights and turn them into your local recycling center for the copper. This is a Win, Win, Win! Be safe and make sure you have your parents' permission to get on a roof or ladder.

35. Baby Sitting

. . . .

This is a proven method for making money. Babysitting is a great way to earn extra money. Try it with a few new twists. Instead of babysitting, how about playing with kids. Sometimes parents need to get things done around the house and having someone there to entertain the young ones is a great investment.

36. Cleaning Houses

. . . .

This is also a proven way to make money. Everyone needs help with cleaning.

37. Computer Tech Tutor

. . . .

Technology is changing all the time and the very young and old are left in the dust. Offer your knowledge to the elderly and very young to teach them the basics on a computer, email, Facebook, etc.

38. Build Doll Houses

This can be big money! Go to new construction sites and ask the General Contractor for extra supplies and build doll houses. Take your time and make them good and all the little girls will want one! You can even build a mini skate parks or car parks for the little boys. Sell these door to door or on-line.

39. Neighborhood Theater

. . . .

Get all the kids in the neighborhood and work as a team! Pick a backyard where you can set up a stage. You will need actors/actresses, script, stage crew, and a leader. Put on a play for the neighborhood. Charge the parents to see the production and sell refreshments at the play. Make sure you include as many kids who want to participate. This means more families to come and see the show!

40. Make Book Marks

You can make book marks out of many different materials. Get creative. Then try selling these at local book stores, libraries, or schools.

41. Water Indoor Plants

Keeping up with watering indoor plants is hard work for any busy family. This is one chore that seems to get neglected the most. Offer services to come each week and water, sing, talk to the plants, and keep them groomed. Plants area alive and need love and attention. I'd hire you to water my plants!

42. Face Painting at Birthday Parties or Other Events

. . . .

Are you an artist? Offer your services at farmer's markets, events, parades, community gatherings, birthday parties, Halloween, and more! Kids love their faces painted and will pay money to have it done. If you are new to face painting, try picking only a few designs to master. Slowly learn more designs and add to the selection. Have Fun!

43. Build Lemonade Stands

How many little kids do you see on the side of the road selling punch or lemonade? What about building lemonade stands? Keep it simple and make sure there is a place to attach a sign. Sell them to kids in the neighborhood or online.

44. Construction Site Clean Up

. . . .

Do you live near new construction homes? This can be good money especially if you keep all the usable materials such as; wood, nails, shingles, drywall, paint, cement, etc. Charge for the clean up and then keep the materials to make other things to sell. Double Whammy!

45. After School Programs

Create a place for young kids to come after school to do fun or educational activities. This can include, homework, recreation, tutoring, playing, babysitting, or work shops to help kids with specific things such as; Safety, Strangers, Bike Safety, The Truth about Tobacco, Service, etc.

46. Brushing/Feeding Horses or Other Animals

Are you good with animals? Offer your services to local stables or families with animals. Feed, brush, and care for animals. Do this weekly and create consistent income.

47. Assistant Coach

There are many children sport teams and many coaches who need extra help managing their team. Whether you are helping with the equipment, practicing with the team, or helping with the managing of the team, this can be a good way to make extra money.

48. Personal Life Guard

Are you a good swimmer? In addition to adult supervision, it's comforting for a parent to have an extra set of eyes to help watch their children in the pool. Charge by the hour.

49. Take Little Kids Christmas or Special Occasion Shopping

Wouldn't it be nice for not even the parents to know what their getting for Christmas from their kids? Have the parents drop you off to a store, give you a budget, and then you can help the child shop for their parents. This will be fun and exciting for both the parent and the child. Then, help the child wrap the gift.

50. Weed Bouquets

One of the most beautiful bouquets I made was out of weeds. Gather all types of beautiful weeds and put together unique bouquets to sell for Mother's Day or Valentines Day. Wrap them in clear wrap and add a pretty ribbon. Sell them door to door or on the street corner.

51. Write a Book

. . . .

Who better to write a children's book than a young person? You understand what grabs the attention of a young mind. Use your talents to write and illustrate a book. You can self publish or submit to publishers. This can be a very fun way to make money.

52. Sell Firewood

. . . .

When I was 14 I noticed one of my neighbors cutting down trees. I asked if I could have the fire wood, bought some industrial strength wrap, and packaged log sets. Over Labor Day weekend, I sold all the firewood for $5 a bundle to people camping at Yuba Lake in Utah. Is there a popular vacation/camping spot where you live to sell firewood or ice?

53. Build Bird Houses

. . . .

Spring and Summer time is a good time to use your creativity to build bird houses for front porches or gardens. You can design it yourself or look for some patterns on-line. Sell them door to door and include bird feed for an extra fee.

54. Build, Paint, Put Together Model Cars or Airplanes

Are you more mechanical or artistic? Try putting together model cars or airplanes and selling them to the parents in the neighborhood. Make an example of one to show, and then allow the customer to pick their model, colors, etc. Charge up front for the materials and then allow enough time to put it together. Collect the remaining money on delivery of the model. You can even sell these on-line.

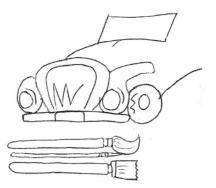

55. Parent Paid Education

All parents want their kids to learn and if there was a way to get you to focus more on education, we'd do it! Ask your parents to pay you for putting puzzles together, reading books, mastering educational games, etc. This will help you find a little more motivation to do the things that will sharpen your mind.

56. Sell Candy, Water, Drinks, and more at Parades, Baseball Games, and Other Events

Get a wagon, put a cooler and other treats in it, and walk the pavement selling stuff at events in your community. Check with your parents to see if you need a permit.

57. Water Lawns

Do you live in a neighborhood where the yards don't have sprinkler systems? This is great news for you! Set up a schedule to go around the neighborhood and water lawns, plants, flowers, and gardens. This will keep your neighborhood pretty and help neighbors to not leave their water running over time.

58. Take Pictures and Video's at Children's Events

Every parent loves to have pictures and video of their kids playing sports or performing an art. Take a camera and video camera to these events and record and snap pictures of the event. Then go home and use your computer to edit the video or pictures highlighting the different children. Next sell these videos and pictures to the parents of each child. You can email the video and pictures or transfer it on a DVD for their library.

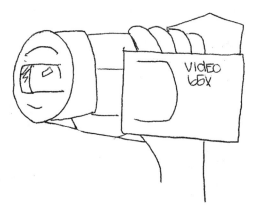

59. Read Books to Little Kids

Offer a book reading service to the kids in the neighborhood. You can do a story time for all, or go to each client individually to read a book of their choice. This will help the kids and give the parents a little extra free time to get things done around the house. If there is a kid in your neighborhood who needs help learning to read, you can do that too!

60. Clean Out Garages

How many garages need a good cleaning job? Go door to door and charge by the hour or by the job to clean out and organize garages. This is a big job which equals big money.

61. Patch Boats

. . . .

Do you live in a community where the kids have inflatable boats? Great! Set up shop to fix the boats with holes in them. You can even buy old boats with holes in them, fix them and resale them. Place a local ad on-line to find these boats.

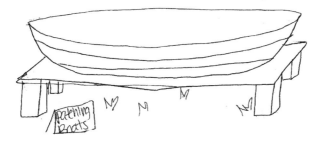

62. Refinish Old Bathroom and Kitchen Cabinets and Resale On-line

. . . .

Place an ad in a local classified paper or on-line offering to take old cabinets from old houses. Then take these cabinets refinish them, put new handles and other fixtures on them and then resale them on-line. You will need who ever is donating them to drop them off to you or have a parent help pick them up.

63. Build Go-Carts and Sell Them

Are you good at building Go-Carts? If not, learn! Build and design Go-Carts and easily sell these to the kids in the neighborhood or on-line.

64. Acting/Modeling

There are many kids who make money acting in commercials or modeling for print ads. Your parents will have to be on board, but this could prove to be a great way to make some extra money.

65. Neighborhood Newsletter

What's going on in your neighborhood? Highlight different members of the community, place ads, or cover neighborhood news each week. You can make a newsletter each week and sell a weekly subscription to your neighbors. You can even charge to have someone place an ad. As you build momentum you can expand your neighborhood boundaries. Start small and build from there.

66. Refereeing

Sign up with your local Rec Center as a referee for children's sports. You can make extra money while you are young, and keep doing this your entire life if you like it!

67. Create your own You-Tube Channel

Did you know that You-Tube can be a great way to make money? You have to get a lot of viewings, but once you do, You-Tube will pay you to keep it going. There are kids making money doing all kinds of things such as; instructional, entertainment, or funny videos. Have fun and keep your fingers crossed.

68. Forex Market/Stock Market

You never are too young to start learning how to invest. Forex.com has a free 30 day trial and tutorials on-line. Stocks are easily bought through many on-line stock broker services. This one will take some training, but you can do it! Look on You-Tube for free videos to teach you this business.

69. Aerating Lawns

· ·

Rent an aerator machine from a home improvement store. Go door to door and offer to aerate lawns for a reasonable fee. Do this in early spring and mid fall for the most success. Try finding your clients beforehand so you know how many days or hours to rent it for.

70. Washing Windows

· ·

When I was 13 years old, I bought some window cleaning equipment and went door to door washing windows. You will have to learn how to take out a screen, use a ladder, and of course clean a window. Practice on your own house. Charge by the window.

71. Gas Station/Store Runner

Do you live near a store or have a bike to ride to one? You can charge parents in the neighborhood to do gas station or store runs. Out of milk, eggs, or just craving chocolate? You can go get these things for families in the neighborhood on call. I'd hire you all the time!

72. House Sitting

Are you responsible? Offer your house sitting services while your neighbors are out of town. You can take care of animals, water plants, turn off and on lights to make it look like someone is home, or simply keep an eye on things while they are gone.

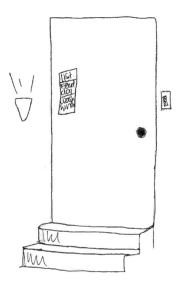

73. Kid Olympics

Organize a neighborhood Olympics with different events. Then charge parents for entry, and sale drinks, snacks, etc at the games.

74. Simple Mechanics

Are you mechanical? Try offering simple mechanic services to your neighbors like changing oil, air filters, spark plugs, or anything else you are good at. Make sure you know what you are doing! And ask permission from your parents first.

75. On-line Store

You can sell anything online. So why not have an on-line store selling stuff you have made, refinished, or bought in bulk? You can do this on Amazon, ebay, through local ads, or on Facebook. I'm sure there are many more ways too!

76. Morning Car Warm-Up/Window Scraper

Do you live in an area where there is extremely cold weather? Set up a morning route with your neighbors who go to work early and go scrape their windows, warm up their cars, and then keep an eye on the cars until they leave. They will surely enjoy a warm ride to work.

IDEA #_____

Description_____

Total Money

Earned_____

Materials/Equipment

Cost_____

Time (Hrs.)

Invested_____

(Money Earned) - (Cost)/(Hrs.)= Profit Per Hr.

Profit Per Hr._____

How much did you make per hour? Is this a good way for you to make money?

IDEA #_____

Description_____

Total Money

Earned_____

Materials/Equipment

Cost_____

Time (Hrs.)

Invested_____

(Money Earned) - (Cost)/(Hrs.)= Profit Per Hr.

Profit Per Hr._____

How much did you make per hour? Is this a good way for you to make money?

IDEA #_____

Description_____

Total Money

Earned_____

Materials/Equipment

Cost_____

Time (Hrs.)

Invested_____

(Money Earned) - (Cost)/(Hrs.)= Profit Per Hr.

Profit Per Hr._____

How much did you make per hour? Is this a good way for you to make money?

IDEA #_____

Description_____

Total Money

Earned_____

Materials/Equipment

Cost_____

Time (Hrs.)

Invested_____

(Money Earned) - (Cost)/(Hrs.)= Profit Per Hr.

Profit Per Hr._____

How much did you make per hour? Is this a good way for you to make money?

IDEA #_____

Description_____

Total Money

Earned_____

Materials/Equipment

Cost_____

Time (Hrs.)

Invested_____

(Money Earned) - (Cost)/(Hrs.)= Profit Per Hr.

Profit Per Hr._____

How much did you make per hour? Is this a good way for you to make money?

IDEA #_____

Description_____

Total Money

Earned_____

Materials/Equipment

Cost_____

Time (Hrs.)

Invested_____

(Money Earned) - (Cost)/(Hrs.)= Profit Per Hr.

Profit Per Hr._____

How much did you make per hour? Is this a good way for you to make money?

IDEA #_____

Description_____

Total Money

Earned_____

Materials/Equipment

Cost_____

Time (Hrs.)

Invested_____

(Money Earned) - (Cost)/(Hrs.)= Profit Per Hr.

Profit Per Hr._____

How much did you make per hour? Is this a good way for you to make money?

Printed in the United States
By Bookmasters